Tadpoles Find the Sun

Allison Grayhurst

Table of Contents

No Gods, no Heroes,
only women and Hector

The misdirected vengeance of Hera.
Grey-eyed Athena's wrath and jealousy,
and Dionysus, bringer of merciless punishment -
(feral mother ripping the limbs from her son, unknowingly,
but when awakened, an internal bonfire grief
beyond extinguishing.)

Hector was the only noble hero -
shouldering his course and obeying his love.

Crafty Odysseus tossed baby-Astyanax
from the towers of Troy.
Crazed Achilles knew only the fury of his passion
as he flooded Scamander with the cut-up corpses
of his mad-rage.
Ajax the Great impaled himself in service
to his affronted ego, and Ajax the Lesser - a coward rapist
of the prophet pure Cassandra.

Give me one-eyed blindness, stay on the path, past
Hecuba and her wild rivers of unfathomable suffering -
childless when once a mother of many, Queen
of an honoured realm.

Give me Electra over Hera
with her young-woman's devotion
and subterranean heart, tied to a father
that would have killed her as he did sister-Iphigenia
on the pyre-offering of war, victory and fame.

Give me a settled glory - my God of Mercy instead
of candles, Jesus instead of Apollo's
thick sensuous thighs or golden curls,
demanding matricide of Orestes.

Give me Helen in her betrayal of red-haired Menelaus,
Helen, daughter of the Swan, lover
of pretty-boy Paris, Helen,
mascot and scapegoat of war, but never the cause.

Give me Clytemnestra over Agamemnon, daughter
too of the Swan, bearer of a mother's authentic wound -
Iphigenia lost on the bloody rock
by obeyer-of-Zeus, mighty-father
Agamemnon's royal hand.

Zeus, kind only to sycophants,
Zeus, serial adulterer, user of woman,
sire of many children, lusting as the sunlight lusts
for Earth, to seep warmth into her crust
and heat up the whole of her surface,
demanding offspring life.

Give me Penelope over
teller-of-tall-tales, Cyclops-outwitter,
slaughter-of-suitors Odysseus.
Penelope, with her patient intelligence weaving,
unweaving, keeper of fidelity
for twenty years, holding her own
up against the plight of a woman's, even a Queen's,
accepted inequality.

Give me steadfast Antigone,
crowned by an ancestral curse,
champion of funeral rites,
brother's defender, daughter-guide,
caregiver of a doomed once-king,
embracing her savage fate with magnificence.

Give me poor Io, chased in her heifer-frame
from flat plains to cliff ridges
to Prometheus's cursed crucifixion to
finally a resting point in Egypt -
Poor Io, ancestor of the brute-blooded Hercules,
who claimed madness-by-Hera turned him
into a murderer of his wife and sons,
who was no Hector, only
undefeated.

Give me Andromache's zodiac-fingerprint,
for she held Hector inside the cavity of her loins,
and he loved her, and for a time, they both knew
happiness.

Because

Because there is a child,
there is infinity and grace
like a grape, crushed, filling the
senses - exotic abundance.

Because there is love between lovers
the broken shelf doesn't need replacing,
the pond can dry up and no one will lack fresh water.

Because a mother's love has no limits,
it stretches past darkness, obstacles,
remains fierce and tender at once.
She knows herself less important than that love and
all else perishes beside its glowing depths, worthless.

Because when others fail in love, God does not,
picks up the slack - gives promise like a shield or like
a bucket full of rainwater.

Out of chaos the primitive gods were born -
divinity separated to be comprehended, grasped loosely.

Because there is one God,
because there is Jesus - hands, feet -
the threshold of freedom in eternity.

Root yourself here. Tie the ribbon.
The ditch is now a road.

Because of mercy and forgiveness,
mercy as forgiveness,
         we all have won.

Sand

Kick the tree.
The tree is a bone
cut out from the Earth.
Jump on the pavement and crack
it with the force of your rage.

Withering is not an option,
white-knuckling it
at the hidden horizon is keeping
you alive.
But it is futile, an out-of-tune song
wrestling for a harmony it will never find.

Praise the shellfish, the moles underground.
A world of faith is forming on your tongue -
you can taste it, but it is not enough
to satiate.

Release desperation and the anger that follows.
Feeling imprisoned was your default position
when being shepherded into reality.
Now you are new like Adam and like Eve
you died in brutal increments
and in brutal increments
you are being reborn from time,
unlike Adam, unlike Eve.

The stream you see is a blessing. The wind
is all around, and sometimes when listening,
it is faraway instruction. Other times,
it topples you over from its reeling power and at that time
you know for certain God is God

and there are no substitutes or shortcuts
or sure-fire prophecies
that will ease the fear of unknowing.

There is just that wind that says
'Go here' 'Go there' and when there,
maps out
an unexpected direction.

Centre-Faith
(while dreams swirl all-around)

Soothsayers and seers and shamans
have children, have the same
rising and falling stars,
cannot say "This is truth"
"This will happen"
There is only God's voice in the now,
leading to the next step and only
that step until the voice comes again.

Even in times of constant accepted prophecies,
the intelligent threw their crystals,
took notes of the pattern
but balked at the interpreters.
Journeys to the Navel-stone were daily -
whore-kings and crushed-citizens
sacrificed animals and even slaughtered
their own offspring
on the advice they were told.

But God is one
and God is permanent
and us,
being tied to time,
are not privy to visions into the future, no vision exact -
we are all equally blind, and that blindness
is a gift that opens the door to faith,

free-falling in our days,
fortunes and misfortunes,
arms open to God's ways and grace,
open like a painter choosing his colours
like a poet, her words.

Open
ecstasy in the listening,
surrender in the execution,
gleaming, gloriously summoned
into immediacy, into an all-demanding
autonomy.

A Dream Suspended

Sinking in the void, held by
nylon line and my eye sees nothing
but that void, cannot turn to the
sunny above or straight ahead to
the insect landscape and daffodils.

So the void spreads and sprawls, and then
starts to whisper - touching the shadow
to my skin, making promises
that haven't even begun their manifestation.

Visceral futility stronger than fear
as I dangle over that blank-space reality,
and there is pressure like living gravity pulling me,
tensing the hold, wanting me to snap
and plunge into pure nothingness,
become the state of vacancy, have no frame,
no barrier or beating pulse.

It is winning, I hear
the creaking
with even further taut suspension and
my weight grows, nearing that midnight twist.

A dream suspended that has my whole future in its hold.
So I call out for help like I have many times before.

Do I strike a match, pretending it is a star?
Hang like the tarot hangman over that dull and ruthless ache,
swing a little and I might feel the possibility of a breeze?

      I dreamed myself untied and running, sometimes
      skipping, brimming with a joyous equilibrium.

      I dreamed there was no void, only a place
      of still-time, a purgatorial interlude as I shift
      from this flow into another.

Light that came

Light that came
from the unending grief -
black-hole of pity sphere,
riding, sucking in, swirling
doomed to perpetual collapse.

Light that came
from hours caught in madness,
thrashing in the ribbon-tied, lock-chain
shadow centre - vacuum plague, persistent
as a wild current and just as impersonal.

Light that came
and broke the shell,
reached in and lifted, lifted me out of
the drowning water. That light is
a cold mercy, a sharp sword as my only defence -
detach - slice the limb that offends and watch it
bleed with indifference.

Light that came
to a changeless darkness changed
everything once maimed
so it could walk again.

Light as a miracle, whispered -
don't give hell power,
separate yourself, cage it,
and when you feel ready,
kiss its forehead, sing it a song
- lullaby, lullaby.

Glory, believe

Glory, believe
the evidence is clear,
brought to a boil and
now boiling over.

World molested by greed,
indifference and distraction.
The pitch has elevated to burst
the eardrums. Scavengers are
scavenging and nothing is left.
Old ranks topple, protection is
a thin veil, fear overcomes prayers,
prayers that kept us sane.

Children and animals are the new Earth's aristocracy,
Bless this time of turmoil - setting
everything upside down, right side up.

Jesus still walks the barren roads,
sandals in one hand,
at ease with whatever is to come.

Let me walk - a servant
yet absolutely free to not serve.
Let me make an oath to the celestial night,
an oath to replace panic with faith and
uncertainty with light everlasting.

I see the light everlasting,
the wheel that is not a wheel
but a sphere.

Exit Door Closed

Down
because the flame is still holy
but the moon's cold cloak
has won.
Leaning into the crossing over,
sweet exhaustion, the love of
absolute rest.

Is this what the fish feels
after minutes on the hook, on the dock,
or the rat gasping in the trap,
lunging, flailing before finding
the peace of death?

Fear is not a name, keeps no company with surrender.
Holding the reset rose in my hand. I see colours
that please me, the brush stroke of renewal
and a house true to its inheritance.

Every hero eventually dies,
and their mourning is made
into a ritual.
Light of God, kinder than a mother's wing,
richer than the formation of a new constellation.

My arms are enough,
even my meagre successes seem sufficient,
infused with Your light,
taking away the pressure of existence,
keeping pace with duties
and the honouring of dreams.

Stark Relief

      Blundering, in disguise -
a gift masked in disease,
tongues imploring forgiveness,
love tested at its roots, glorious
as mountains.
      Boredom and fear meeting in unison,
finding a strange fulfilment behind locked doors,
venturing to walk in the open air, take hikes,
sit by the lake-waters and dream, alone.
      A gift that doesn't carry a typical joy,
but breaks down the superficial slaughter
of what is truly meaningful, simplifies the one thing,
the all thing, that connects and is worthy of attention.
      Love in illness, love at death, love in gratitude
for the lifeforce we have been given - its sacred mission,
not meant to be plundered on distraction and greed.
      God is the only safe ship left to climb aboard on,
the only ship afloat on this burning sea.

The gift has come, and yes like everyone,
I am afraid. In my mind,
I join the people singing,
raw in mutual fear and faith,
a collective voice, harmonized, joined
from balcony windows.

The light has gone out.

Nothing is plenty or even sufficient.
The door opens, but there is no escape
just the long wait under an isolated sun,
walled up in fear and deficiency.

It could have been completed, sealed
into the account but darkness hammered
the blush from blooming, and yes, the lesson
to see was written on the Stonehenge, in
the past lives in an ancient Athenian tribe or
when setting five-alarm fires on the moon
when you were a golden muscle, ripe
and violently ending anything soft.

Greed gave you all the cards, opinions that
lacked a spiritual dimension. It will not come
until this ecstasy is laid flat.

You see - O Tantalus!
You see the stain that created your torment, unearthed.
Walk on it, shed its blood and let it bleed out
its deeply embedded drive and expectation.

Hell is individually formed,
a private backyard betrayal.

Walk into the shower,
let it cascade down and dissolve this last
unseen-before glitch - see it, wide-eyed
and say 'forgive me' say it and
be free.

Rationed

Ration out the unified soul,
make it many instead of one.

See the breakdown of what is holy,
split into particles
uncomplimentary, wasted.

Trust in the brute because he has
no self-doubt, no self-examination,
Because it is easy to sacrifice
autonomy for certainty
and slice the swan's wing
for monetary gain.

Before the circle became a line, some
nutshells still held their core - arguments were
for the sake of reflection and deeper knowledge.
When the circle became a line, tyrants were given
free-reign - the mutual exchange
between fear-and-getting replaced morality.
The ones of lights passed away
passed over their passion, replacing
faith with conspiracy theories.

Describe this gift of life.
What does it mean to you?
There are many waves,
one water
equality within the hierarchy
value in no-control.

Death is automatic
but choice
        no God
        yes God
is always

        an open door.

Open Wide

On the table, the whole of humanity
burning with fear, this onslaught
of harm, but love is not the victim.
All who have a soul within them, end up
rising up to meet the challenge of justice
and compassion.

The few who died long before their death
are now indisputably barren
and frighteningly corrupt.

Acts of mercy, acts of grace -
all of us deciding
which side we believe in.
All of us are now citizens, heroes of our charge,
children of the divine, effective, more
than helpless, feeding off God's mercy, day to day
hour upon hour - held hostage to our inner world,
stripped of superficiality and distraction,
called to claim the slaughter we are accomplices to -
to choose the resting-nest of gratitude.

We are all asked to perform doubtless music,
formulate our morals and digest them
like a cure we have no choice but
to adhere to

for the horseman is at our tails and his shadow
is hard upon our shoulders.

Deathbed

Strength has changed
appearance, ends with a mask,
begins with food of only a humane source.

In the late winter I built my nest,
made a cradle from branches and waited.
Now that spring is over and no offspring came,
I consider this cozy island a curse,
feel the heat approaching and have no joy to give.

Upstream, blood soaked in debt and weapons
I cannot wield, weapons
on the floor, by my feet, too heavy to lift.
I embrace the dread like I once did grief - inhabiting
my days with failed effort, trying to dull transgressions,
manage my Sisyphus rock
- push for the prize that never comes - push,
believing it will, knowing it won't.

My barren longing, unremarkable, repetitive.
I would change my name, my shape, if it would help,
grow plumage where there is none,
but my energy is crushed with clinging,
and the freedom that lords before me
like an oasis is only finished fiction,
a book of great magnitude, but
foiled of substance and lasting nourishment.

Build

By the whirling heap of fate
a new being is born - one that
watches, moves and holds.

One that stands without future plans
or regrets but takes two days to make
a decision and then sticks with it, in spite of
contrary opinion.

Blood on the knees, covering the unborn joy
that does not know if it can withstand the first breath,
but still kicks its way out of the womb.

There is nothing easy here on this planet,
its sharp beauty cuts and bends everything living
to the cruel unpredictable violence of survival.
Collapse, famine, or warm nest out of the rain -
the same parallel process of dying and becoming.

Standing noble when in weakness,
or succumbing to slavery
is the only vantage point choice.

Touch your eyes,
touch an outburst of sorrow,
touch beautiful geography underfoot.

Faith is a house, takes you in
to live sometimes as part of the furniture,
sometimes as a carpenter,
making furniture, sweeping,
making more furniture.

Mercy without Miracles and Miracles without Mercy

A day 2,500 years ago
and life was the same, struggling
to understand God and fate
and how the stars may hold
prediction but lack all means
of mercy. For mercy
was an evening without power, was weak
as was seen
the majesty of forgiveness.

It was before Jesus came as sibling, as friend,
revealing the depths of God's grace, the redemption
in surrender and late evening devotion, breathing
with the direction of the wind, open to hardships
as to miracles, orchestrated by a loving hand.

First God was many in our minds,
segregated, dissected, tangled with human
hypocrisies, pride and jealousies.
Then God was one in our minds,
higher, mightier than death, closer still,

until

Jesus

let us hold God in our arms, be held like
a tiny flower head is held by a child's hand,

cupped, yellow buttercup, glowing,
treasured by God, each of us,
a necessary and loved creation.

Back then, even great minds glimpsed
such profound greenery,
but could not complete the joy.

Jesus is
humanity's completion with God,
connection, void of complications,
like an infant's first smile or that infant,
growing, learning,
holding out her arms,
saying your name.

Water Wings

Taking off my water wings
soon
maybe in a year or two,
maybe in ten
I will front crawl
fast to the edge, go under, somersault,
push off and speed,

or climb the high diving board,
up the steep metal steps, gripping
tightly, half-way there to the edge, three quarters then
race and leap, arms outstretched, thumbs locked and
going down, hitting the water fast, gliding across
the whole of the deep end.

Letting go of spiritual infancy, primitive
magic-tricks that sometimes worked,
most of the time, didn't,
to soothe my anxiety, needing
the evidence of God, instead
of trusting faithfully, fully
- water wings off, front-crawl free.

Wind – Marrow – Bone

Death comes softly
like a small wave or
a blanket, lessening
the stroke. Slowly
the energy leaves and also
the will power to not let it go.
Death is gentle as a spider's steps
or like the innate laws of decency
methodically, incrementally, ignored.
Death, I rejoice in you, as I didn't know
how easy your touch was or how
pain and weakness arrive like your welcome mat.
Unless you arrive violent, but then, that too,
because it is quick, is merciful.
Bravery on the altar where you are worshipped
where you demand every part of a soul unseen to be seen,
equal parts of cowardice and courage, the darkening whine
and the warrior who makes it up the stairs
when the body's strength is but a secret, barely
audible, straining to be heard.
Death you are tender,
you ready us for the quiet nod - yes
or the scream that ripples across the ocean - yes!
You make sure to narrow us completely
so you are the only way out, and we want out,
we want you - like a lover - Death,
lover of the drowned, the burned,
the cancer ward occupants, the accident fallen
and illness that compresses the lungs,

topples over the perching bird.
          In the end, we all want you,
jealous lover of the living,
you take us all
either with a breaking virility or
smother us in a maternal fold.

Beautiful Death,
I have come close to you
and I learned
you are made of love,
embracing completely,
sensuously,
in the final surrender.

Prometheus Speaks

Prometheus speaks
from my bathroom tiles, wailing
his defiance and fiery nightingale burning
with his tongue still unrooted
and his limbs bound to the rock, spread
like wings - Titan of the windfall, humanity's
hope and champion, more brilliant than
his dumb and primitive siblings, more committed
than their arrogant and willful offspring.

Prometheus in the shower curtain, dripping
liquid fire down the drain, plunging
into the underworld depths
then up for a greater torment to meet the predator bird,
dispelling all screams and ghosts and holding tight
to his suffering-throne and his compassion
for such a flawed creation.

Prometheus finally rescued
as the warm water exerts itself from on high,
- strong Herculean flow -
the wounded centaur accepting his fate.
Flow Prometheus,
trustworthy, burning, speaking
your conquering gospel,
the first crucifixion
the first flame ignited
before love's great inception.

Dying, an echo

Hardship harder than
the unprotected inferno I fell into
that has sealed above.
No courage will raise me out
of its burning cavity,
its lava-ruin grief pressing down
like a great wave of heavy water.
All that's mortal in me is sick, subjected
to this bright and furious master.
All that is immortal in me has gone silent,
its sails clipped, its joy orphaned and emptied.

What happened?
How did this take me, pull me
into its unbearable heat so fast, so frozen,
draining my life-force with its hot poison,
leaving me no option of flight?
How did I become an exile of all I held sacred,
hardly walking up the stairs,
every breath a banishment from life,
every resting position, a pressure on my chest
like an anvil coming down, down
and staying its weight, concave?

What do I see? Nothing. Value
has turned to ash.
Love holds my hand but cannot release me
from this hell.
I wake up and prayers have failed me,

all my understanding has crumbled
like wafer chips of dried-out clay -
eagle broken, sliced up on a sharp rock.

Bird

Up into
a wet pillow cloud sky
bird of flame
like a yellow rose
touching the toes of gods,
past treelines and skyscrapers,
daughter of the wing,
receiver of the mating dance.
Bird beyond laws and names,
the visionary's touchstone,
keep your flame and rise
like love rises and engulfs
the blooming darkness or like water rises
devouring the whale-hunter's boat.
Up into the firmament,
higher than the experienced stars,
your craft is art, your light uproots time.
Do not land, but keep rising, a gold dome
over the blue, answer every dream
with a glowing !yes!
be our temple and our immortal hope.
Bird
absent of grief or longing, bird of flame,
you are smooth, loose and pliable as
the flesh of deep eternity.

Hell Seen

Unseen, the darkness is a tsunami gateway,
engulfing every fragment of will,
builds unexpected, a shock of water filling
the lungs, chaos infesting every corner of the mind,
rational thought on fire, cindering, seared by
loveless insanity.

This is the inheritance that must be thrown overboard,
tossed like a corpse that is plagued with a contagion.
No room for sentimental mercy which is not mercy,
only a longing for comfort that in the end
compromises protective barriers that must be upheld.
All ties must be cut and loyalty to God,
the only link left.

I visited hell, shadows grabbing my every corner of flesh,
loneliness like an amputated limb,
released and thrashing, abandoned
from its fertile blood source.
I was afraid, every cell drenched in horror.
I had no voice, no substance.
I was shown hell, experienced hell
a flood, a plummeting down down

Even in that evil landscape,
my loved ones saved me,
prayers said outloud saved me,
and the haunting loosened its hold.

Now seen, I see
there is only God or hell -
God or
anguish, anxiety, blunt force destruction,
pounding torment, a rotting waste.
God and
life embraced,
a rapturous and difficult glory.

You Open Your Mouth

You open your mouth and
I am gone again like
before I could walk, like
before I had anything but you
and this connection, gripped
in a violent spin, intimacy purging gravity
by free will alone, blood for food and food
tossed on a gravestone, seeding a graveyard,
lording triumphant over reality, more potent than
waiting for the streetcar in a cold sub-zero winter,
waiting with wet boots and uncombed-through hair,
like fruit that never spoils
or gets polluted with scented-hand touch.

You say destruction
and I am beating the light,
slashing the torpedo into
smaller precise devises of doom.
You say reconciliation
and I am beside you, planting
my vengeance like dead peeled skin,
like waking and walking
to the bathroom, leaving the dream behind.

You open your mouth and
you open a door to a feast
outstripped of butchery and good cheer,
outshining all but the lover's volatile love pitching,
emerging, continuing, clear,

Breastplate

With this breastplate
forged in the fires of tangible Hell,
I will go forward, doling out
gifts that God entrusted me with,
feeding sparrows, starlings and squirrels.

I will command my days with a mature discipline,
more so tied to the wind in a place of freedom,
boundaries set by my soul.

Everyday I will eat and be grateful.
I will leave my licence plate in the gutter,
travel light like I did when I was younger,
one knapsack for years - live in this home
but claim no possessions. I will listen,

pitch my tent in any wood
as long as the birds guide me there,
and I will keep myself breathing,
full of breath -
active, on watch.

I will love, love like I do
with a personal intensity
the ones that feed me with their love,
keep me in grace and breakdown the shadows.

With this breastplate I will go,
for I know how evil consumes

in small amounts with small yeses,
small indulgences that grow into
a vast hole.

I will wear sandals in the summer,
a jacket in the winter and this breastplate,
now grafted to my skin,
willfully dreaming this journey forward,
surfacing uninhabited shores.

Hector

Shining Hector
Man-killer Hector
Hector, prince of the walled city,
lover of loyalty, prized invincible,
devoted, never set adrift by lust or changing distractions.

Hater of war Hector
Warrior Hector, protector
of a worthy ideal, a harvest of fulfilment,
wealth for all, raining down from your native desert sky.
Husband on a private balcony, holding time still
for declarations of love as the flooding
enemy-army neared,
gathering its hero-giants and enraged half-gods,
sealed in indestructible armour.

Hector, son of Queen Hecuba and King Priam, brother
to reckless sweat-hearted Paris.
Father of an infant babe, Hector,
who feared death like every other, ran and was chased,
then finally stood alone, willingly, facing his murderer,
knowing the result like knowing the lunatic gods, how
they etch out each mortal's destiny
on the inkpad of their erratic whims.

Never marked or bruised, your corpse above ground
for eleven days, still fresh as when your soul first departed.
Your father begged to bury you, winning this small mercy,
you were buried, sacred rites restored.

You were mourned for your perfect beauty,
(their defender lost, their defeat inevitable).
You were loved for your strength,
the kind derived from clear-cut purity,
a rare internal moral code.

Glorified, the tale of Hector,
outliving millenniums,
outlasting countless other heroes.

Hector of the soft dark hair, golden helmet, shining.

Wings

Continue dreamer, down the halls,
through the citadel,
gather wings in your arms - small ones,
medium ones, feathered and translucent.

Follow the mini-current across the line,
then rush through forbidden lands,
drop those wings and wave your arms,
sing loud, sing ugly - nothing is a branch
that can't be broken, nothing is a swing
that can't be stilled.

Far away, in the ocean's depths
there is no visible sun,
no use for warmth or a changing horizon.
The bird is condemned
in those depths and your voice
is just a bubble.

Rush to the edge of the shore
and decide your fate, glittering surface all aglow,
confined on land or in the water?
Take a step forward or
turn around, commit absolutely
and move.

Continue dreamer, down the halls,
listen to the warnings,
swallow them into your gut and
test your courage,
gather those wings and rush.

Cliffs

I died every day
on the sorrowing cliffs,
a wolf pack closing in,
things I knew and believed in,
ordained, then tossed over the edge.

Prophecy was nothing, and shelter and bread
connected to this tortuous trope,
turned comfort upside down and spat
upon my flush face with all the vigor
of a personal enemy.

I fell asleep near the cliffs, woke up and wondered
why I was left here - still alive, no rescue in sight -
thinking of a helicopter, an angel, an army of
hunters or even a large helium balloon
to grab onto and ease my descent.
But I stayed near the cliffs, hearing the pack,
seeing their eyes through the undergrowth
but never feeling their jaws at my flesh
and never crossing the barrier into the abyss.

I stayed on the edge and waited as though I was
already in my grave, and I thought - is this
a purgatory punishment? A loop etched in linear
time, a fire on my back that burns and burns
but never consumes?

I am not sure if I am sleeping.
I am not sure if I am truly alive or a ghost
destined to repeat an unending horror,
wandering through the same torment.

I am ready to see, close my eyes, nearer, nearer, and leap,
be dashed into fragments or be vindicated, either way,
relieved.

Onslaught Cloud

When courage is smoke,
and it takes far too much effort
to build a mound to stop the flood,
        when fears and the bleeding winds of reality
destroy the indestructible diamond, turn it
into dust particles, lapped up
by the tongue of unsuspecting animals,
and the storm, it digs a wound like a valley,
red and brutal,
        when that happens, it is time to sleep, dream
of better days, watch TV, read and listen
to other people's stories,
bury your battle-slain heart under the covers and wait
for meaning.
        Meaning when found will restore courage,
sooth the raw chasm, give faith in the setting sun
and maybe even
press up against you, thundering,
a glorious beauty.

Pretzel

This prayer was the last prayer
devoured and regurgitated into a lie.
Hearts I voted on
desired safety above courage, avoidance
above truth and speculation above action.

Two-fold was this falsehood, this
pollination of pitiful love.
Drug-induced, polluted with vagueness
and amoral substitutes for honour.

I believed in you, comforted you
in your wanderings and in your torture.
But this river has gone undernourished,
dried into a barely moving stream.
What was grand and glorious,
a life source for a whole ecosystem,
now strides without gusto or usefulness.

Liar at the full moon.
Liar when you hide in your fantasy,
and then you lie again and hiding it,
say it does not count but it counts,
each lie builds a bed, littered with compost,
bars that block the view from the sky.

Everything I thought was strong,
unbreakable, deathless,
has ended in this infestation,

as you play-act queen light warrior,
indulging in ego-feeding conspiracy theories,
harming truth, defiling acts of other people's courage.

So much suffering, whitewashed,
arrogantly dismissed, by you,
doubtless in your cult-convictions,
saying 'awakening!", building platforms
on top of platforms -
a grotesque paradigm of crazy,

where you have all the answers
and I have nothing left
to hope for or to say.

Dissolved

A weighted shadow was on my back,
triumphant, feeding off of me
in day-to-day thoughts,
dealings at the grocery store,
getting dressed
and walking.

It flourished its victory everywhere I went,
in the judgement of strangers and the shame I bore,
wearied by reality.
It was thirsty, thirsty for the substance of my faith,
feasting on the debauchery of my despair and in that feast,
it grew four times its original size,
cementing my wings in permanent collapse.

Now this weighted shadow is dissolving, swiftly
in glorious movements of clear! clear! clear!
It has not gone completely yet, but I am stretching,
able to raise my neck and strengthen my shoulders.

My fears are painless, grace has entered
and brought the promise forward.
Under my eyelids shapes are forming,
ones I have never known -
tribes of mighty animals and
communities of celestials.

We say hello.
We walk on the fresh born grass,
and the grass morphs into a mountain,
with a valley,
with a river.

So Far

So far the winter came
for 22 years, steps taken
to burn the past failed
like speaking, washed up on silent shores.

So far I lived with eye drops
from the river of honey
stolen and then savoured.
The Earth's cord was tied to a heritage
of fear and inevitability - children
with beaten upon organs, panic, grovelling
at the feet of survival, so far.

So far, the miracles came
and covered my breasts with oil,
softening my hair with almond milk,
saying - this is enough - so far.

Half of the day I was tormented,
half of the day I was in bliss,
in a private heaven full of secret doors
and perfect-shaped rolling hills,
watching my children grow, loving
and learning from my Apollo-love husband
of the lyre and bow and arrows, riveting,
slicing the dead wood, bringing both burn and joy.

So far I have not been on many airplanes,
have stayed most days indoors,
feeding those children and animals
of rich personality and anomalies,
enduring some, mostly,
nourishing, being nourished.

Now I am drinking solely from the sky,
releasing the tether of gloom
and penetrating the center
without the leftover madness
of senseless suffering.
Cracking the shades of oblivion, released
by a gift that was always coming
and by the grace that has carried me
so far.

Simple

The darkness crashed
on a sapling morality,
cracked pretensions and then hope.
It was two-fold, folding the
young visionary and the tired warrior -
into one power, depleted, elapsed.

It weakened a once flourishing joy, skillful
in its demise, necessary for what was
born after - compassion in harvest,
a home well built
on any hard or soft shore.

Raise the clock, break its hands,
snatch immortality from the arms
of culture.
Tiny dreams are gold. Trust in those dream,
even more golden.

Fast, faster in the circle -
run of linear time, gleam fastest
at the summit
at the nadir,
and commit to only love.

Take a Tree

Take a tree
and its bond to the Earth,
its spell upon the sky
its stretch and swing among the squirrels.

That tree is all trees,
powerful without a pulse,
slow to hunger and slow to react.
It sleeps when it wakes,
receiving its action even when in full bloom.

       Somebody climbed that tree,
wanted to build a fort but didn't,
just sat between a strong forked branch
and looked across and down.
       Another touched that tree, its crust trunk,
the folds and curves of its sensual permeance.
In that touch was found a different measure of time,
a way to stand back and wait for growth.
In that touch was a shifting,
deeper than meditation,
connecting below and above rooftops.

Take a tree, in any season, at any time of the day,
the alien dimensions it moves between,
its response to the moon.

Knock on that tree softly and it will open.
It will greet you,
invite you in and show you a place
without dance, without disorder -
primordial creation, a wellspring-confidence,
a dream   that has no dreamer.

Times

Sometimes
I am dropped into evening's glory
beside you, relieved of cunning, anxiety,
at peace with the dried nest cupping a crushed egg.

Sometimes
it is forward
and the wind that is wild is on my side
gathering forces to aid in my direction.

Sometimes
I am single, cloaked in
a dazzling and lush solitude, plump
at the core.
          Roots are wings and those wings
          never suffer fractures or deformities
          but are final in their perfection.

Sometimes
I ask for just enough
to be guided from my prison cell
to build a lasting fire and have food
for my children.

Sometimes
I know I am loved
and those times are the best times -
infinite voices to chose from, colours
everywhere and heaven tangible,
inside my sheltering home.

Temple

Expanding, raw and pulsing
like newborns that grow into
individuals of their own
from one source
of everlasting literature.
From a cave of damp demise or
from violent fires, stoning heroes, forging heroes,
never quite sure who the enemy is.
From a journey of fantastical obstacles,
no mistakes made to stop and graze
and settle for anything but home.

Others have felt this eternal wealth of inspiration,
drank at its well and spoke -
making more riches, forests where feet
can travel and be in awe.
And from those others, still more have come -
one line flowing from the beginning.

O Ilium and Ithaca!
The same stars spinning.
Our beautiful Earth rest in you -
devotion, cunning and courage.
Love matters, but these things
which are the actions born from love
matter more.

Your fire is bright, brighter than
your ancient sun, has rhythm, repetition,
has harvested a hymn, etched permanently
in the foliage of our collective souls -
strong shoulders, driftwood, the first breath-cry
poet-bard.

Cost

When you bleed
do you bleed in the summer,
early morning, on wet grass?
Or just because the door is open,
do you close it and walk up a steep hill?

When you are walled in, is it prejudice
or wisdom, packing you tight, with no
left-over spaces to stretch?

Each day comes like a sword, living is charged
with complexities that must be cut through -
amputated calcifications to reach the fleshy core.

I thought we could sail straight through the waters
but you, lover of chaos, called in the mad waves
and rode them gleefully to any shore.
I can only catch up,
follow and accept your choices.
I can only ask myself -
what fresh boundary must I break through?
What deep-set morality must I re-think?

For love, for you,
to keep us true, connected.

Which Way?

      Blue I wondered
blue in summer in
the mornings, caught in
the snail-size tales of
futility and inevitable floods.
      Crooked boundaries, solid as
vapour, stung, trapped my fears
far from knowing the mercy of self-forgiveness.

I carried my purse like a stone, collected
empty wrappers, useless pens
and expired medicine,
burning always from head to foot,
impatient for change,
running into the concrete walls
of my collected fate.

Today, I look at the bloom of yellow flowers,
full in their last burst of joy before the frost,
and I am learning to drop that stone,
accept what lives and what cannot.

My bitterness has lost its vein to travel through,
forms and then corrodes.
Let others count their dollars
and covet extravagant houses.
I love my home like a trusted friend

and my garden is a portal into heaven
where the robin drinks and the mange-bitten squirrel
has made her home, digging, storing nuts.

Throats are cleared.
God's giant voice has won
my full attention.
Switch me off. I am ready
to swim far into the ocean, fast
until my lungs burn, desperate for air.
There I will stop (the shoreline visible, but barely).
There I will wait for an answer, recover my breath and
decide - further out or back home.

Hand

I bore the yoke,
surging against the assault,
counted the thin space that buffered me
from disaster.

At the beginning there was obedience
but also the certainty of great heights.
After years of being unable to stretch,
there are no more prophecies or ranks to aim for
or glory for a future horizon.

The unknown is dense and impassable
as a steel sealed curtain.

Maybe here I can learn what Jesus always knew -
that prayers are speeches of the greatest importance
but listening holds more sway,
that obedience to God
is the only currency-exchange, must be
the authority of each steps taken,
is the root determination of peace
or anguish.

The first time I held out my hand,
I expected tangible abundance,
fruit, seeds, candy.
Now I hold out my hand
and hope only
to keep it open.

The air is light, causing no pressure, no trembling.
It is easy in its emptiness,
lacking anticipation, lacking
a future, past comparison.

Sister Lost

A sister lost
to a mad-weave calamity,
hanging off the platform,
an ego-dream of dumb self-importance
- the war on truth that
masks its face as though it were truth,
but is only a gate to an easy explanation,
a system of hellish accusations and propped
up pillars of false justice, combating fake forms
urging anger forefront, poisoning
by such a sure promise of victory.

I send you sleeping sister. You say
I am sleeping and you twist your conspiracy theories
into a cloak of great magnitude, condescend,
so confident of your place of holy honour.
You jumped over the mark, missed it
and plunged into an upside-down dream of realty.

Once, a sister, a comrade,
an unbreakable bond, broken.
I cannot see you. You cannot see the evil
you have wrapped in fool's gold,
claiming righteousness
as you measure your worth
by this aggressive attack on truth, denying
the wind, a child's cry, a mother's redemption.

Sister, I loved you, I still do,
but you have crossed the line.

It is terrifying to watch.
It is a shock to finally see
who you have become.
You took the plunge
long before I accepted your choice.

By your choice, your inner conflict
became an accelerant bile-fire,
you became a plurality, parts, parts
condemned to feed off
intellectual Jell-O,
find entertainment, immaculate purpose
in unbalanced passions and impulses,
claiming a cure by creating a disease.

Pythagoras-Ovid Royalty

Unwed from heritage,
for the tie of tradition is darkness,
and the price in the folly of lineage,
is a line to cross, to be born into
but never earned.

Sink or swim in your history,
families are special
like all families are special, like
all cultures are beauty mingled with cruelty -
things that hardened into meaningless rock
and things that are allowed to move
and keep their lifeforce.

Be born like a new babe,
eyes set on only mother-father God,
don't carry the price and the agony of your blood
that is only blood, not spiritual, and only mighty in illusion
by you ordaining it so.
Belong nowhere and hold that freedom
that is hard to own and is immediate
as a mountain is
or a rainstorm.

Race with the wind, lighten the burden,
bathe in a burst of ever-fresh glory,
toeing the line for no one - release
all wounds and accolades
of what you claim as your own
but where and who you've never been -

If past lives are real, then belong to every
race, every culture, every species.

Once we were all fish, so
stop fishing.

Doorway

Feet are flesh
and have been flesh
for thousands of years.

        Saying wisdom is fresh
is the vanity of a present-age.
Better minds have spoken before,
challenged their own authority and
didn't take death as seriously as
we do.
        Keeping honour was the only
crucial wealth, reciprocity and
the graciousness from host to guest.
        Mothers loved and mothers grieved
with same weight of worry of motherhood,
and lovers held hands, wishing for great blessings
to match their great love.
        Music was poetry and poetry was
the greatest gift of all bestowed, poetry
to keep humanity sane, stretching
further into the heights of immortality.
        Feet wore sandals, raced across
Mediterranean shores. Hands
were always hands too,
beautiful, complex, useful.
        Healers were rock-like with equal
shadows and solidity, attached to the earth,
rituals woven from the lion's breath.

Warriors too, took their virtue from
the mountains, climbed and often leaped -
breaking bones, arresting their pulses, lusting for fame
and a good afterlife.

My feet are soft like many who have feet I know.
Compassion still counts as the highest offering
offered from one to another.
The suffering of one resonates,
relatable across centuries -
a doorway-understanding
to the suffering of all.

World Away

World away of hollows
where light escapes, gets
through, flourishes in the
sluggish dream of humans.
World of many layers - up
to pure communion and down
with the languishing un-animal beasts.
Rivers that flow and merge, travel down.
Oceans rise up, their surfaces new,
surfaces discovered - air, sometimes just
air, other times, divine space where eyes
can come close in, examine the stars.
World away of purple and gold,
merging lava with its harmony above.
Thorns that wake the many sleepers,
places where forgiveness is the only escape.
Stones are mirrors, their surfaces blurred,
their boundaries unmasked and glorious flowers are
eternal.
World away where the faith in money
is a mouse-trap, catching souls, keeping them there,
broken and anguishing.
World above of pure worship
and simple communion - smells move like lust,
desires amplified, approved,
like electric current-catalysts
for standard-accepted-forms of fulfilment.

   Colours of elms and of eagles, everything
less thick and less challenging.
Heads up, love
the obvious go-to solution.
   World away of patchwork tunnels,
going down, going up, a journey
matched in the imagination -
many dimensions, many limitations
added or lifted.
Moon half. Moon whole.
   World away where
walking forward with truth at the helm
is the maker of glory,
a living lucky charm.

White Butterflies and a Red Squirrel

Influences deserved
never arrive, and
the gift remains in the pocket
like chapstick on a cold day,
or as bits of sharpness to remind you
not to get too comfortable, complacent
or convinced of your rigorous calculations
when you calculate the sides of a square,
a triangle, an oracle reading.

People you thought would never go,
have gone, walked away
from sanity's reach, most likely never to return.
Things you wish would have left years go, remain,
your days outstanding, tied to the
root-whip survival, lashing.

And there is more never expected -
a banquet of nourishing literature,
a husband still coalescing with brilliant light,
two children grown, kind and weaving,
and the animals, older, happy
watching the birdbath in the flush garden,
in a backyard that in the early morning
as you scan the interior and the perimeter,
you are sure that nothing could be more glorious,
pleasing, leaves you praising
for being allowed to witness such royalty.

God's love heats up your pores,
fills your nostrils with green scents,
fills your ears with the chatter of communities -
sparrows, starlings, bumblebees, white butterflies
and the red squirrel. You are sure
such kneading, thinning-thickening harmony
is the natural state of being,
propelled to experience this nirvana, (spinning, spherical)
knowing tomorrow it won't last, but also knowing
it will always last, existing, uncorrupted,
sealed, continuing in this moment, this morning,
this day, in this exact summer.

Communion

A snail is a slug with a shell,
is like a hand with only one thing to claim,
was like my thoughts that leapt out of a stream,
fell on land and could not get back.
Old life
like a spider caught in quicksand,
gone into the murky underground.
Worry was a cavity,
a reservoir endlessly re-filled,
scooping up a cup, resolving a problem,
as old problems grew larger to fill the space
or infant ones formed.
Leaving the dramatic spinning wheel,
mending the wounds of sacrifice.
How long before the thirst to satiate
is satiated, then becomes thirst again,
greater than the first longing?
Why is there heat everyday and never rain?
Is time just the planets rotating
like spherical untouchable gods, or
is it nonsense, divisions made
for small minds to draw imaginary
pathways through stark oblivion?
When I learned
Jesus walked with his arms open,
his hands empty, feeding, being fed,
then I arrived in God's grace
as though I had always been there.

My past was relinquished,
incorporated like a candle flame
into a larger fire,
into the greatest summit.

Ambrosia

Light feet
feathered longing
between a grazing herd
and the grand appearance of peace.
Dreams arrive, slide in like a knife
to reshape reality, denying
blood spray, the ripped winter coat,
stories that die untold.
Add the nectar, symbolisms of jumbled-up
joy - a dog's smile, a run through the forest,
tie it together like a housecoat or an idea that has
lingered without reward. And there,

fate is waived
for a stronger endearment, choices
are made that shock the natural order.
Love is understood as an act of the greatest courage
and bodies change, transform their elemental structure -
wind becomes sea, stone turns to air.

All guests are rested and fed through his metamorphosis,
things that disfigured and imprisoned are blessed
for the strength and moral clarity that they gave, then
like dreams, they are kissed gently,
remembered when first waking, then
while brushing teeth, they are
gone.

The Night Before

I praised and held the wind in a jar.
All the while, the stars melted, old gods
were replaced by new ones, and the once invincible
were fated to run lunatic through communities, terrorizing
and leaving pathways of blood with their strong arms
and war-loving minds.
          Dancers curled up like centipedes,
poets lost their poetry to analysis and clichés,
and worst of all -
no one was able to tell the difference between
what was gold and what was a trinket.
          My hair was long, back then, I remember,
my beaten-up hands were supplicating,
but every blessing was denied me, from weariness,
from loss and from my own hard-hearted pride.
I was ready to be fatally wounded, as such an ache
would an adventure.
I was ready to run across a river
and test the currents' force against my own resolve.
          So I went north, away
from the wicked heat Mediterranean sun.
I praised, and in that praise, was half-way perfect.
A mouse could not know my skilled imagination
and an eagle was too high to tap deep into my shadows.
          I went up a mountain, but first over
that river. I sang a new language when
I touched the snow, sang,
making an Eden in that virgin toil.

Mid-air

I reached across the riddle-barrier,
shaved my head and walked through the door.
I took my clothes out of the closet
and burned them,
I watched the light dim all around
and walked over a cliff.

I did this without a choice, only a decision
to embrace a movement forward.
I was commanded to do this, and I consented,
not without struggle and self-loathing,
not without fear and a sense of deep failure.

Now I am falling, I am in the air, eagle-spread,
a sharp pain in my side and the wind whistling
its rapture.
Everything people do
is bound to kill them eventually.
Take dancing or bricklaying or being a mother.

I am still falling, I have not landed
in someone's arms nor on the sharp rocky bottom.
The pain remains, so does the wonder,
as I fall, falling,

Advance

Leave this place,
it is for beginners
and the ground is an overgrown
outside used-to-be sanctuary, trapping
you in its weeds.

Be steadfast as a revelation
years after being revealed, infused
to your intelligence, supplying water
and detachment when necessary.

Walk through the ruins then jump the fence
and do not relapse into nostalgia or a thousand
what-ifs that have no viable conclusion.
Pull the plug, cast away what was once
a masterpiece but has since degraded,
orbiting a dead star.

It is easy as taking off a coat on a warm day.
It is dialectics and you are at the nadir,
traveling the circle around, soon to rise.

Leave what you cannot afford to keep
as it is too invasive a burden
and you are ready to expand, stretch out,
canopy a richer domain, permitted
to be fully nourished and explore.

Crossing Over

Crossing over into
a porous aftermath,
a root-return basket
of exposed veins and ligaments.

It is sad to be like a lung
that cannot fully expand, but good
to open a window and appreciate a breeze.

When I quit feeling responsible
for what I am not responsible for
I will be free to sort out my assets
and impressions, structure them into
a viable source of fodder and food for
all who I love.

      When I wore a uniform,
I thought myself the whole army.
      When I wore the monastic robe,
I placed myself at the mouth of the void
and whispered to myself achieve! achieve!
      When I walked with no arms,
only legs, no language, I thought boldly in block colors,
in over-exposed senses, smelling indisputable exactitudes
like insects mating in tall grass, and fish
rotting on the river banks, and even the sun
had a smell, its fragrance dependant
on the season and its placement in the sky.

When I lived without a body,
lived as part of the swing-loop-spin cosmos,
formless and yet whole,
thick and thin,
curved and straight, sensitive
without the possibility of being wounded,
I knew crossing over
was treacherous.
I chose to cultivate the separation principle
and see if I could return to unity.

The body is a tale, the rest
has no account to record.
I filled my flask. I died fighting
and also when surrendering.

The law will never be known,
only fragments of the law, a maturing of,
and maybe even inclusions, after a long
century time.

Jesus is water flowing, limitless like heaven is
in vitality and truth.
All I must ever do is guard that connection
as the only thing sacred - everything else
that is irrational, rational
or cohesive or unleavened or supplied
will make contact but be redundant,
be imperfect, and leave
a longing, insatiable.

About the Author

Allison Grayhurst is a member of the League of Canadian Poets. Four of her poems were nominated for "Best of the Net" in 2015/2018, and one eight-part story-poem was nominated for "Best of the Net" in 2017. She has over 1,260 poems published in more than 490 international journals and anthologies.

In 2018, her book *Sight at Zero*, was listed #34 on CBC's "Your Ultimate Canadian Poetry List".

Recently, her work has being translated into Chinese and published in "Rendition of International Poetry Quarterly" and in "Poetry Hall".

Her book *Somewhere Falling* was published by Beach Holme Publishers, a Porcepic Book, in Vancouver in 1995. Since then she has published sixteen other books of poetry and six collections with Edge Unlimited Publishing. Prior to the publication *of Somewhere Falling* she had a poetry book published, *Common Dream*, and four chapbooks published by The Plowman. Her poetry chapbook *The River is Blind* was published by Ottawa publisher above/ground press December 2012. In 2014 her chapbook *Surrogate Dharma* was published by Kind of a Hurricane Press, Barometric Pressures Author Series. In 2015, her book *No Raft – No Ocean* was published by Scars Publications. Also, her book *Make the Wind* was published in 2016 by Scars Publications. As well, her book *Trial and Witness – selected poems*, was published in 2016 by Creative Talents Unleashed (CTU Publishing Group).

Collaborating with Allison Grayhurst on the lyrics, Vancouver-based singer/songwriter/musician Diane Barbarash has transformed eight of Allison Grayhurst's poems into songs, creating a full album, "River – Songs from the poetry of Allison Grayhurst" released October 2017.

Some of the places Allison Grayhurst's work has appeared in include Parabola (Alone & Together print issue summer 2012); SUFI Journal (Featured Poet in Issue #95, Sacred Space); Elephant Journal; Literary Orphans; Blue Fifth Review; The American Aesthetic; The Brooklyn Voice; Five2One; Agave Magazine; JuxtaProse Literary Magazine, Drunk Monkeys; Now Then Manchester; South Florida Arts Journal; Gris-Gris; Buddhist Poetry Review; The Muse – An International Journal of Poetry, Storm Cellar, morphrog (sister publication of Frogmore Papers); New Binary Press Anthology; Straylight Literary Magazine (print); Chicago Record Magazine, The Milo Review; Foliate Oak Literary Magazine; The Antigonish Review; Dalhousie Review; The New Quarterly; Wascana Review; Poetry Nottingham International; The Cape Rock; Ayris; Journal of Contemporary Anglo-Scandinavian Poetry; The Toronto Quarterly; Existere; Fogged Clarity, Boston Poetry Magazine; Decanto; White Wall Review.

Allison Grayhurst is a vegan. She lives in Toronto with her family. She also sculpts, working with clay; www.allisongrayhurst.com

www.ingramcontent.com/pod-product-compliance
Lightning Source LLC
Chambersburg PA
CBHW051803130726
47987CB00003B/1089